£20

Gordon Beningfield

Best wishes

Gordon Beningfield.

Gordon Beningfield

This is the cottage in which I have lived with my family since 1974. It was built between 1540 and 1560. Apart from the dormer windows, which are a later addition, it now looks very much as it might have done then. When I bought it, though, it had white lime-washed walls and black beams, and if the inside had not been so dilapidated it could have passed for pre-war mock Tudor. It took many hours of painstaking work to restore it to something like its original appearance. Behind the cottage, separating it from the old orchard, is a thick hedge of large hazel trees that bring nature right up to the windows of my studio. At the front, the marshy and uncultivated land that stretches down to the river Gade (and the view that I have painted for the endpapers of this book) is covered in summer with thick and luxuriant vegetation that has never been sprayed with horrible chemicals and provides a perfect breeding habitat for many of my favourite butterflies, not to mention all manner of other wildlife.

Gordon Beningfield

THE ARTIST AND HIS WORK

VIKING

VIKING

Published by the Penguin Group
Penguin Books Ltd, 27 Wrights Lane, London w8 5tz, England
Penguin Books USA Inc., 375 Hudson Street, New York, New York 10014, USA
Penguin Books Australia Ltd, Ringwood, Victoria, Australia
Penguin Books Canada Ltd, 10 Alcorn Avenue, Toronto, Ontario, Canada m4v 3b2
Penguin Books (NZ) Ltd, 182-190 Wairau Road, Auckland 10, New Zealand

Penguin Books Ltd, Registered Offices: Harmondsworth, Middlesex, England

First published by Viking 1994
10 9 8 7 6 5 4 3 2 1
First edition

Filmset in Centaur by Cameron Books, Moffat
Reproduction by Brian Gregory Associates, St Albans
Printed in Italy by Artegrafica, Verona

ISBN 0-670-85197-3

Edited by Jill Hollis
Designed by Ian Cameron
Produced by Cameron Books, PO Box 1, Moffat, Dumfriesshire dg10 9su, Scotland

Illustrations Copyright © Gordon Beningfield 1994
Text Copyright © Cameron Books and Gordon Beningfield 1994
Design Copyright © Cameron Books 1994

A CIP record for this book is available from the British Library

The picture on p.49 appears by gracious permission of Her Majesty Queen Elizabeth The Queen Mother.

I am indebted to the following for permission to photograph and reproduce works for this book: Dena Bryant and Terry Duncan, Mr and Mrs Norman Gerard, Mr and Mrs Ronald Gerard, Mr and Mrs Nicholas Halsey, Mr and Mrs James Herbert, Mr and Mrs Anthony Hoare, Mr and Mrs Harold Hughes, Father John McCoy (Church of the Holy Family, Welwyn Garden City), Mr and Mrs Alisdair MacGregor, Christopher Parsons (Green Contract Productions Ltd, Imax Natural History Film Unit), Royal Mail, Mr and Mrs Derek Saunders, the Reverend Jeremy Sheehy (St Margaret's Church, Leytonstone), Mr and Mrs Roger Smith, Solomon & Whitehead, Unicover Corporation, Sir Max and Lady Williams, General Officer Commanding Household Division, Commanding Officers of the Regiments and Chaplains of the Guards Chapel.

Paintings on pp.58-59 © Copyright 1984, 1991, Unicover Corporation, Cheyenne, Wyoming, USA 82008-0001. All rights reserved. Reproduced by permission.

For assistance with this volume, I am especially grateful to: Sergeant Fred Barrett, Bruce George, the Gear Family, The National Trust, Port of London Authority Museum.

Many people over the years have helped or encouraged me in my work, but I am particularly grateful to the following: Clare Alexander, Caroline Baker, BBC Natural History Unit, Bert Beadle and Faithcraft, Eric Bedford and the Old Boys Committee, Mr and Mrs Henry Bedingfeld, Chris Beetles, Mr and Mrs Edward Beningfield, Mr and Mrs John Bridges, Dena Bryant and Terry Duncan, Mr and Mrs Brian Booth, David MacDonald Booth, Simon Bowes Lyon, Burlington Paintings, the late Robert Bush and family, Sarah Caisley, Ian Cameron, Mr and Mrs Colin Carr, Derek Christopher, Peter Crawford, Thomas Crispin, Mr and Mrs Thomas Dean and family, Brigadier and Mrs F. De Butts, Professor Dr and Mevrouw W. DeLoecker and family, Mr and Mrs Phil Drabble, Roy Faiers, Mr and Mrs Brian Fensome, Mrs Stella Ford and family, Mr and Mrs Dennis Furnell, Mr and Mrs Ronald Gerard, the late Frank Golding, Mr and Mrs Robert Goodden, John Groom and family, Dr Peter Harper, Miss N. Hartley and the late Miss A. Linton, James Helzer, Mr and Mrs James Herbert, Mr and Mrs John Heyward, Mr and Mrs Ron Hickman, the late Juliet Hill, Jill Hollis, George Ingar, Brian Jackman, Jennifer Jeremy, Mr and Mrs Bill Jesty, Tony Lacey, the Hon. Lady Lyell, Mr and Mrs Royden Marriott, the late Eric Morecambe and family, Robin Page and family, Mr and Mrs Richard Pailthorpe, Mr and Mrs Barrie Parrott, Christopher Parsons, Shaun Payne, Mr and Mrs Richard Pearce, Roger Peers, the late Roland Richardson, Barry Robinson, Vivienne Schuster, Mr and Mrs David Shepherd and family, Peter Shrives, Mr and Mrs Ian Smith, Mr and Mrs Roger Smith, Solomon & Whitehead, Mr and Mrs Alan Southgate, Diana Toms, Peter Ward, Dr Peter Ward, Mr and Mrs Peter Westgate, Ronald Wigley, Mr and Mrs Roger Wilmhurst, and all my friends at Water End.

THIS BOOK IS DEDICATED TO ALL MY FAMILY

Works Illustrated

Family Album

My parents, George and Emily Beningfield, around the time of their marriage in 1926.

Above: my parents in the garden of my uncle and aunt's house in the late 'thirties, and me at the age of four in Bermondsey. Below: with my parents and my younger brother Roger, who is ten years my junior, at London Colney around 1954.

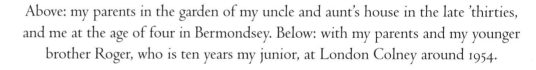

My wife, Betty, in about 1974, when we moved into the cottage where we still live, near Hemel Hempstead. Being an artist is not the most secure of jobs and sometimes involves taking risks that would alarm many people, but Betty has always given me the most tremendous and unwavering support. She has dealt with mountains of correspondence, wrestled with VAT returns, helped me with exhibitions, discussed ideas for paintings, in short she has been the most reliable and trusted helpmate I could possibly have hoped for.

My daughters and our dogs in 1971. Sally, aged nine, is with our first Scottish deerhound Rory. Sarah, aged five, has her arms around our border terrier Snuff, and our very first dog, Jane, a crossbreed, is in the foreground. Because of my own passion for the countryside, I was determined that my children should have a rural upbringing. From when they were about two years old, I used to take my daughters out with me on expeditions with the dogs. Of course, once they had grown up there were all sorts of distractions that were more exciting than the countryside, but it was soon clear that they would always come back to it.

Early Years

For a long time, my family lived or worked within sight of Tower Bridge. My maternal great grandmother lived at Horselydown, close by the bridge on the south side of the river. When my mother, together with her brothers and sister, went to visit her, they often saw oil paintings sitting on her easel, though I think they were more interested in the shilling she used to give each of them every Sunday. The day the bridge was opened, exactly a hundred years ago this year, my grandmother pushed my Auntie Ann across it in a pram. Some thirty years later, her daughter, Audrey, in turn distinguished herself by getting her head stuck through the masonry as she tried to look down at the river, and a policeman had to be called to get her free.

Like many of the other men in his family, my father was a waterman and lighterman. As soon as he had left school, he began a seven-year apprenticeship on the river. The indentures by which apprentices were bound in those days were pretty tough and affected your whole life: among other things, you had to be in by a certain time in the evening and you weren't allowed to 'frequent taverns'. My father's master was his elder brother, Alf, and when he came to the end of his apprenticeship, he had to pass what sounds a bit like a very severe driving test: he had to navigate a lighter single-handed down the river, through a number of bridges, and, of course, across the busy Pool of London in the middle of the working day, all under the critical eye of his brother who was following behind him in a tug. He and his brother, together with

a senior lighterman, his Uncle Bob, hired themselves out much in the way that threshing gangs did in those days. They would get contracts with, say, Hays Wharf or Butler's Wharf, and as cargo came in they would ship it from warehouse to warehouse along the river. The company that owned the tugs they used had given all of them the names of insects, and the one my father always talked about (and even drew for me) was The Gnat. There was a lot of work around in those days for skilled watermen. My father's wages would have been about £12 a week, but there were times when he could earn as much as £40, which was a lot of money and the reason why he could afford a car when they were still pretty uncommon.

When I visited the Port of London Authority archives recently with my family, we were shown a number of photographs of the working traffic on the Thames in the 1930s, and there, miraculously, was one of The Gnat. I was so delighted that I decided to paint a reconstruction of the kind of scene my father would have worked in, when the Thames was a hub of enormous activity and the focus of so many people's livelihoods, rather than the deserted place it has now become.

I was born in my maternal grandparents' house, which was in one of the marvellous late Georgian, early Victorian terraces that were so enthusiastically knocked down in the 1960s. In 1939 my parents moved into a new flat in Bermondsey. With rather surprising foresight, the block had been built with two underground bomb shelters, and by 1940 we realised how fortunate we were to have them. On many evenings that year we went down there, fearing bombing raids. Then in September 1940 there was a colossal attack on the docks around the Pool of London. Many of my parents' friends and some of our relatives were killed and a lot of bombs dropped on the area where we lived. One evening, when I was in the shelter with my mother and some of the neighbours, my father had just turned up through the door with a tray of tea for everyone, and a landmine hit the road just outside. The blast threw him right off his feet, and there was tea everywhere. The actual shelter stood up to the impact, but the wall split, and gallons of water started pouring in from a burst water main. I clearly remember the rush of cold air as I was lifted up through the escape hatch and into the arms of an ARP warden under a starlit sky outside. Soon I was being carried by my father to a makeshift shelter under a nearby railway bridge, and a few minutes later my mother and grandmother arrived. I was only four, but experiences like that stay in your mind for ever.

From time to time, my mother and I were evacuated out to the country. We went to Somerset for a week, and to Burnley in Lancashire, where we stayed with an extremely kind mining family. What struck me most there were the cobbled streets and the sound that the clogs made as people hurried to work in the morning. But it was not long before my mother, anxious about my father risking his life every day in the Pool of London, felt she must get back. So very early one morning, before it was light, she got me out of bed, and the next thing I knew we were on the train heading back to London.

The wrecking of the docks meant that by 1941 there was precious little work around, and my father became a fireman and ARP warden. My mother's sister had moved with her family to London Colney in Hertfordshire, and things had got so difficult in London that my father decided that we should move there too. In those days, it was a small village where the main activity centred on farming. Arriving to live there was a revelation to me. Apart from the silence – I was used to so much racket in London – the two things I noticed straight away were the dark, the pitch black sky (I was used to it being red), and in daytime the wonderful endless green everywhere. That glorious impact of finding myself out in the country has never left me. What seems extraordinary now is that we were only 25 miles outside London. Although he was supposed to sleep during the day, because most nights he went into London on the fire engine, my father used to take me off for rides in the countryside, on the cross-bar of his bike, and he used to sketch and draw and paint what he saw around him. Even though I was only four years old, I think that really marked the beginning of my passion for natural history. To start with, I didn't really look at what I was doing, and just tried to copy his pictures, but he always used to say, 'Paint what you see, Gordon, paint what you see', and that was probably the best advice anyone ever gave me. I was to benefit from my father's

encouragement for many years to come. He continued to draw and paint all his life, in spite of enduring many years of serious illness.

I went to the local village school and later to the secondary modern. Most schoolwork seemed really rather difficult to me, though it was no-one's fault. I was good at athletics, played a lot of cricket and enjoyed history. Luckily my history teacher, Miss Hill, was extremely sympathetic. She realised that even though essays were not my forte, I still loved the subject, and she suggested that I illustrate history rather than attempting to write about it – so my history books were full of drawings. My headmaster, Roland Richardson, encouraged me enormously. He too realised there was no point in trying to force me to do something I wasn't capable of, and at the beginning of each week we used to discuss what I would paint next.

The friendships I made soon after arriving in Hertfordshire have proved long-lasting, especially one with the first little boy I met, Eric Bedford, whom I still see regularly. As it was wartime, we tended to find all our own amusements round where we lived. The bridge in the picture above is the one from which my mates and I used to fish for sticklebacks.

When I was a boy, we were released from school for a couple of weeks a year at the beginning
of the autumn term to help on the farms, when extra pairs of hands were needed for countless small tasks. I was in my element then – these were, of course, the days of mixed farming.
We picked red currants, blackcurrants, gooseberries, cherries, peas, Brussels sprouts. Harvesting
potatoes was another labour-intensive job; I spent many hours spud-bashing, as we called it.
Anyone who has done this will remember the back-breaking labour: you had your pitch, the
tractor went up and down the field digging up the potatoes, and the spinner on the back
threw them out onto the ground. Then we all gathered up the potatoes and put them into a
skip. Before you had finished one lot, the tractor would come round again. It started off all
right, but after a while you were on your knees. By far the most picturesque sight was the
grain harvest, though there was too much dangerous machinery around for children to be
encouraged to take much part in it. However, one of the jobs done by children, including me,
was stooking – standing up the shocks in sixes after the combine harvester had deposited
them in the field.

The Peacemaker

Back in 1943, when I was six and had been evacuated to Hertfordshire, a little girl in the village shop at London Colney, near St Albans, asked me to draw something in her autograph book, and what I immediately sketched were Spitfires zooming over a destroyer. Like many people who lived through the war, I have always been completely in awe of the Spitfire – such a marvellous shape, and such elegance in flight. Just the sound of the engine makes my heart beat faster, even now. They were stunningly manoeuvrable. Even in the 1950s, a good pilot could outdive a jet in one. Somehow, I always felt, even as a child, that it was the Spitfires that saved Britain. There were Spitfire Funds (I still have one of the badges that were given out when you contributed), and everyone put their pots and pans out to be collected and made into Spitfires. Whether they actually were or not is immaterial, as it was a morale booster. Soon after the war began, my mother and I were evacuated briefly to Hassocks. The South Downs were, of course, the landscape over which the Battle of Britain was waged, and one day I clambered right on top of a henhouse thinking that this would give me a better view of the action.

When the fiftieth anniversary of the Spitfire was celebrated in 1986, I went down to the festivities at Eastleigh with my brother. It was a special thrill for me because I was fifty too, and proud to share a birth date with such a distinguished invention. I realised that this 'plane had

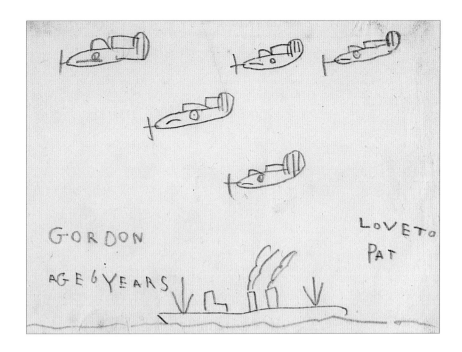

come to symbolise so much to me that I should paint it, and that is how I came to do this study of a Mark II Spitfire, which saw combat during 1940. Just as it was about to be sold for scrap in 1947, someone looked at the logbooks, realised the 'plane's historical importance, and it was presented to RAF Colerne as a museum piece. In 1967, it appeared in the film, *The Battle of Britain*, and it is still flown on special occasions. The hangars in the background are pre-war and derive from archive material at Hendon, as do the lorries and petrol bowsers. One shouldn't forget that the lion's share of the Battle of Britain was taken by the Hurricanes. There were then far more of them (a few are sketched in the drawing below), and the first prototype of the Spitfire had not been developed until 1936. But somehow while the Hurricanes seemed dependable, solid, robust aircraft, and we all have reason to be grateful for their pilots' huge contribution during the war, it was the Spitfires that quickened the blood.

Steam Trains

Steam trains again take me back to my childhood. Wartime evacuation from London, is, naturally, all bound up with trains in my memory. But soon after the war, they became one of the best and most exciting parts of going on holiday, certainly as important as the holiday itself. You would get to the platform, and there at the front of the train was this steaming, spitting, groaning, grunting, marvellous thing that you strained to see before you were bundled into your carriage. The best of the engines had real glamour – like the Jubilee class engine shown here in the watercolour study. No wonder so many small boys longed to become engine drivers.

My schoolfriends and I used to spend hours and hours on summer days sitting up on the embankment above the railway between London Colney and St Albans collecting train numbers, and ticking off in our spotters' guides the 'namers' – the main express engines coming out of St Pancras which all had names. There was such a variety of locos, and the steam just brought everything to life.

The station that appears in the watercolour sketch above is a wonderful example of what has been achieved by a splendid institution called the Severn Valley Railway, that extends from Kidderminster to Bewdley. This is a properly run commercial concern, but its hallmark is historical authenticity. The people who work there wear pre-war railway uniforms, and the care they have taken with details has produced a very atmospheric environment. It's all there: the coal fire burning in the waiting room, the old insignia on equipment, the bicycle leaning against the hedge. Getting on and off wherever you like, having a look at all the bits and pieces in the various stations and, of course, watching the traffic going up and down the line, is one of the nicest ways of spending a day off that I can think of.

The painting opposite shows a Great Western engine drawing into a station. Originally it would have been an olivey green, but it has been painted black because of its transfer to British Rail. The afternoon I spent on the Severn Valley railway gathering material for this painting was great fun. I had gone with my brother and some old schoolfriends, and waited in vain for a train to come into the station in the right position: either it was totally obliterated by another coming from the opposite direction, or it would emerge back to front, hauling its carriages into position. No matter — we had a ready supply of ice lollies and plenty of time to play the fool as though it were forty years earlier.

Ecclesiastical Art

When I left school at 15, my main interest was art, and I was extremely fortunate to be taken on to work in the studios in St Albans of a company called Faithcraft that specialised in ecclesiastical art. I learned to paint, decorate, sculpt, lay gold leaf, indeed to turn my hand to just about anything related to the furnishings and decoration of churches. The training was rigorous and the discipline firm. Soon after my arrival, I remember someone in authority making it quite plain that I was there to work, not to talk. But I adjusted to the regime quite easily because I wanted to learn and was interested. Now I realise that it was an invaluable beginning. I believe strongly that if you want to be an artist, you need to be a good craftsman. Knowing how to handle your material, how to get the best out of it, is one of the most important aspects of an artist's work. I certainly trained in that – from the ground up. For the first few months, I did nothing but wash other people's brushes, mix colour and sharpen chisels.

Faithcraft took me on when I was fifteen, initially to train for five years (though I ended up working with the company for thirteen). Once a week, I went on day release to St Albans School of Art for painting and life classes; I also took evening classes there. For me, the combination was perfect. The dedication and skill demanded by my employers made me realise the importance of discipline and craftsmanship, and the art school allowed me to pursue my interest in fine art.

As I became rather more experienced in my job, I was able to develop some of my own ideas. As long as the workmanship was up to scratch, there was the freedom to try all sorts of things, though it was made quite clear, that if, for instance, I decided to paint the flesh of some figures green, and the vicar didn't like the result, it was entirely down to me. On one occasion, I remember taking a brand new tin of paint from the store, going down to the yard and filling it with earth. We had been asked to come up with an image of the Earth with Christ the King standing on top of it. I started off with a carved wooden globe, then spooned this knobbly mixture of paint and earth and stones on to the surface, covering the whole thing with aluminium leaf so that it looked like a bright, roaring bit of chrome. I started glazing it with enamels to produce a bronzed effect, and finally mixed up a combination of rust-coloured oxides, so that it ended up looking like a chunk of iron. My colleagues must have wondered what on earth was going on, but they just let me get on with it.

Soon I moved to the studios in London to work principally on designs for embroidery on altar frontals and banners and for painted stained glass. A team of lady embroiderers worked right next door – so it was easy to check that what you had suggested would work and watch how it progressed.

Quite often, we would be given jobs in churches some distance away: it might involve recreating a bit of heraldic decoration or restoring a piece of old sculpture. During my lunch hour, I would wander out of the church and sketch it or something I found in the vicinity. The work of John Piper fascinated me, particularly because he too was very involved in church architecture. It seemed natural to try my hand at the style for which he is so well known. The painting opposite shows a corner of Henley-on-Thames with an ornamental public drinking fountain and a Regency doorway that caught my eye over the road from the church.

One day in the bitter winter of 1947, I was walking by St Alban's cathedral with my cousin Freddy (who had been a mechanic on Spitfires and Hurricanes), and we decided to nip inside to warm up – a very welcome move for a schoolboy freezing in short trousers. That was certainly not the last time I enjoyed the hospitality of the abbey.

The shrine of St Alban sums up for me the sheer richness of our heritage in church architecture. It was lost for 300 years in the walls of the abbey, then discovered, and painstakingly reassembled during the last century; recently it was restored to its former glory. There is something enormously reassuring about getting to know beautiful historical buildings. With all the aggravation that you have to put up with in everyday life, it's nice to know that they remain, just as they have for hundreds of years.

Near the end of my time with Faithcraft, my work was in the stained glass studios, and when the commission for a series of four windows at St Margaret's, Leytonstone, came in, I did everything connected with them from the scale drawings of the designs to choosing the glass and painting it. The only thing we didn't handle was the firing of the glass and the leading which was done by an old family firm in St Albans. Three of the windows are shown opposite.

The excellent training I received, for which I shall always be grateful, meant that soon I was beginning to develop my own ideas for whole schemes of restoration for churches and was able to gather together enough private work to start off on my own.

It was while I was at Faithcraft that I learnt how to sculpt. For my own work, I used to buy resin from an industrial supplier, who would have stocked it probably for car bodies. The sculpture would first be modelled in clay so that a plaster mould could be taken, and then the

29

mould was used to cast the final work in resin and glass fibre. For ecclesiastical work destined for exteriors, I sometimes used to pack the mould with bronze powder.

These two works were one of my early commissions. The Church of the Holy Family in Welwyn Garden City was brand new, and I was asked to submit a proposal for a crucifix and for a figure of Our Lady. At the time I was fascinated by Ancient Greek sculpture, especially by the carved drapery that allowed the form of the body beneath to suggest itself. For this figure, the last stage – of toning the leaf with oils – was important in creating the illusion of depth, for this is a bas relief, rather than a three-dimensional figure. For the crucifix, I chose a Byzantine cross – a style that was being picked up in some modern ecclesiastical decoration at the time. The wooden cross is decorated with gold leaf overlaid with oil colour; the figure is glass fibre.

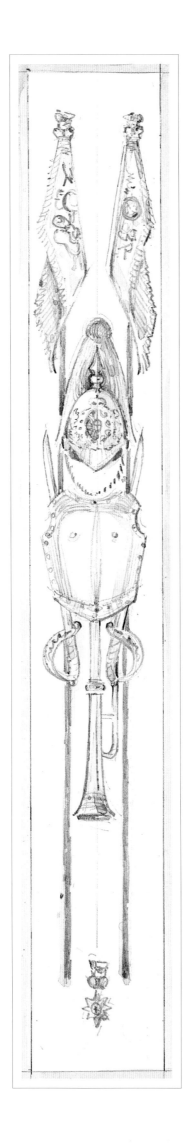

The Guards Chapel

An early commission and one of the most exciting I had to tackle was a memorial window for the Household Cavalry in the Guards Chapel, St James's. When I was approached, I thought they must have made a mistake and were thinking of someone else, and I certainly never thought I would get the job. The brief gave me a free hand to fill a space ten feet by two feet. A trip to Wellington Barracks was organised, and I wandered round searching for inspiration. I ended up in the Armoury, surrounded by silver trumpets and banners and drums, cuirasses and helmets, and realised that these wonderful objects and shapes could form the heart of the design — symbolic pieces of equipment that no one could mistake. I compiled the design, submitted it, and was fortunate enough to be given the go-ahead. And so I set to and began to transfer my ideas to glass in the form of engraving, to produce the window which is illustrated on this spread together with its sketch. Since this window was installed in 1972, I have been asked periodically by other regiments to design and engrave memorial windows, and there are now seven others in the chapel, six of which are shown overleaf — the seventh is very recent. One is decorated with a kestrel because the officer in question was a keen falconer. In another, a flight of geese represents an enthusiasm for field sports.

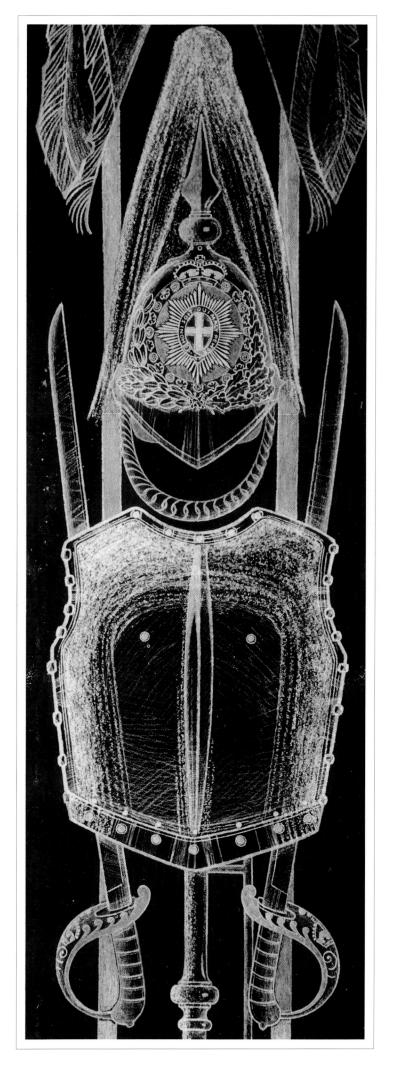

TO THE GLORY OF GOD
AND IN MEMORY OF
COLONEL
DENIS HERBERT ARTHUR LEWEY
COLDSTREAM GUARDS
11ᵗʰ FEBRUARY 1930 ~ 4ᵗʰ OCTOBER 1974

DEATH IS ONLY AN HORIZON

TO THE GLORY OF GOD
AND IN MEMORY OF

CAPTAIN
RICHARD WESTMACOTT
M. C.
GRENADIER GUARDS

KILLED IN ACTION
2ⁿᵈ MAY 1980

WHO DARES WINS

ALWAYS A LITTLE FURTHER

THIS WINDOW WAS GIVEN BY
MEMBERS OF HIS REGIMENT
AND HIS FRIENDS

TO THE GLORY OF GOD
AND IN MEMORY OF
THREE GRENADIERS
KILLED IN SOUTH ARMAGH
21ˢᵗ DECEMBER 1978

GRAHAM DUGGAN
KEVIN JOHNSON
GLEN LING

THIS WINDOW WAS GIVEN
BY THEIR COMRADES

THE GUARDS INDEPENDENT
PARACHUTE COMPANY

PATHFINDERS TO THE AIRBORNE FORCES
OF THE REGULAR ARMY FROM 1948&1975
MADE UP OF VOLUNTEERS FROM THE SEVEN
REGIMENTS OF THE HOUSEHOLD DIVISION
SERVED ON OPERATIONS IN PALESTINE
SUEZ CYPRUS BORNEO AND NORTHERN
IRELAND, DISBANDED AT PIRBRIGHT ON
24TH OCTOBER 1975

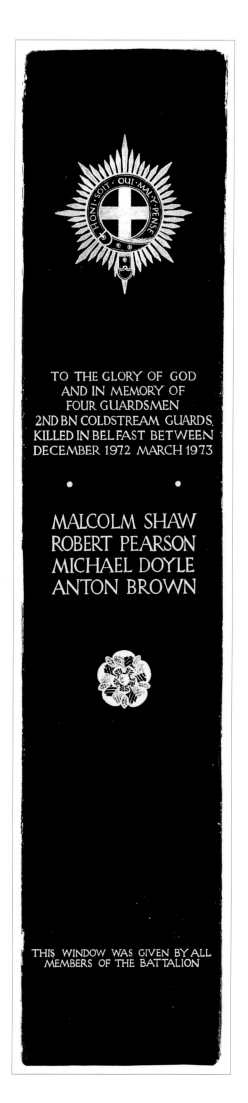

TO THE GLORY OF GOD
AND IN MEMORY OF
FOUR GUARDSMEN
2ND BN COLDSTREAM GUARDS
KILLED IN BELFAST BETWEEN
DECEMBER 1972 MARCH 1973

• •

MALCOLM SHAW
ROBERT PEARSON
MICHAEL DOYLE
ANTON BROWN

THIS WINDOW WAS GIVEN BY ALL
MEMBERS OF THE BATTALION

TO THE GLORY OF GOD
AND IN MEMORY OF
CAPTAIN ROBERT NAIRAC
GEORGE CROSS

GRENADIER GUARDS
3RD JAN 1972–15TH MAY 1977

THIS WINDOW WAS GIVEN BY
MEMBERS OF HIS REGIMENT
AND HIS FRIENDS

Sculpture

When I was about fourteen, I found a piece of holly wood in the school carpentry workshop. There were no gouges, so I hacked away at it with a flat chisel. The result was the little owl opposite. When my headmaster saw it, he decided to enter the owl for the schools section of the Festival of Britain, and we went together to an assembly point for work from Hertfordshire. As I walked through the door, the first thing I saw was a reclining figure by Henry Moore. Never having seen anything like it before, I was amazed, but at the same time deeply attracted to this abstract form. From that moment, Moore's work had a tremendous influence on me, not least because he cared so much about the natural world, and I tried to go to every exhibition of his work that was put on in London. Years later, in 1959, when I was working at Faithcraft, I decided to write to him, telling him how impressed I was by his work and asking whether it would be possible to meet him. Much to the astonishment of my colleagues, I received the most gracious reply, asking me to delay my visit until the following spring when the countryside in which his sculpture was set would be at its best. Wandering in the lovely landscape around where he lived, and just coming across a great sculpture, with the odd sheep grazing near it, was an experience that affected me deeply. Here was art genuinely living in the land-scape. Such was his kindness that the artist spent a good part of the day talking to me about his ideas and answering my questions about his work.

At Faithcraft, there was so much good hardwood used that there was often the odd piece that I could pick up in the joinery department. The fox opposite was something I carved way back in 1955. I can't remember deciding to do it; but even then the subjects I leaned towards in my own time were to do with natural history. A couple of chaps I worked with couldn't understand why I had smoothed off the surface; but I had been reading what Henry Moore had to say, and felt that he was right in suggesting that smoothness gave the beauty of the wood every opportunity to express itself. A lot of the church work I was doing was stylised – for modern buildings – and that must also have influenced me.

The English Longhorns are my favourite cattle. What magnificent beasts they are. Every cow's and every bull's horns are slightly different. Until the early nineteenth century, they were a very popular general-purpose breed. What prompted me to sculpt this group was my book *Beningfield's English Farm*, published in 1989.

Ayot St Lawrence

This is a very special, moving place. I discovered it when Betty and I were courting in 1956. We had set out from Welwyn, walking along the country lanes. It was autumn, and by the time we got to Ayot, dusk was falling. Perhaps that was why it seemed so atmospheric. When we reached the church, I stood there for about half an hour, mesmerised by this romantic sight. In the 18th century, the lord of the manor decided he wanted a Picturesque ruin on his estate (a fashionable idea at the time) and so he actually had part of the church dismantled to achieve the desired effect. Somehow I find the beauty of the architecture merging with ebullient natural growth very arresting; the place has an extraordinary atmosphere. I've tried to recreate the light I remember from that first evening visit in 1956. When I was asked to present an edition of the radio programme, *Down Your Way*, this was the location I chose. The church tower is now in poor repair and a group of people are engaged in raising money to have shoring-up work done so that St Lawrence's magic can continue to work on all those who visit it.

The Countryside

As a young man, I soon grew determined to find a way of devoting myself to painting the countryside. So every bit of spare time was spent exploring and finding new subjects. At first, I tended to paint birds. A lot of my early paintings were gamebirds, because there were (and still are) a lot of sporting estates round where I lived in Hertfordshire. But the two above are birds of prey, a kestrel and a peregrine, that were commissioned by Solomon & Whitehead in the 1970s to be reproduced as limited edition prints.

Opposite is a painting completed this year. One January day, I was wandering around in a National Trust wood, where, against the odds, the dormouse still survives. It's a marvellous, wild place that I often visit with my friend, Dennis Furnell, a writer and naturalist, who shares my great interest in Dorset. There was snow lying heavy on the boughs, the fieldfares were chattering, and there, all of a sudden, was the redwing. For a few minutes there was the curious warm glow that evening can produce after a whole day of cold light. The redwing, a migrant from Scandinavia, settled, paused, and seemed to be thinking: 'Well, this doesn't look too bad – maybe I'll stay here for a while . . .'

Gordon Beningfield

I think I first became aware that the British countryside was under threat in the early 1960s. At that time, I spent every weekend going out, roaming around looking for natural history subjects. Inevitably, I noticed things beginning to go wrong. Instead of working in harmony with the landscape and contributing to the richness of life in it, farmers seemed to be turning the land into a battlefield. As I watched, hedges were cleared out and fields grossly enlarged, woodlands were bulldozed and downland was ploughed up. I almost felt as if I was under attack myself, and it wasn't long before what I was witnessing led to angry words between me and the perpetrators of all the destruction. Straw-burning was what finally tipped the balance and made me realise that feeling outraged about what was going on was not enough; I would have to start drawing attention to what was happening and get people to realise that it had to stop. I don't think many of the farmers even had a clear idea of why they were burning the stubble. There seemed to be some vague notion that they were 'cleaning out the soil'. It didn't occur to them that the soil might be better off left to its own devices. The potash was beneficial to the soil, they explained, but clearly it took only one gust of wind and it all blew away anyhow. Side effects that few of them seemed to consider were the burning to death of countless insects and small mammals like harvest mice and the scorching beyond survival of many hedges and trees nearby.

Not far outside Cambridge is a farm that belongs to the parents of a great friend of mine, Robin Page. Birds Farm is at the centre of a scheme that a group of us have set up to encourage what you might call farming sympathetic to nature. Robin's father and brother have always farmed sensitively, and the idea is to build on their work and extend the farm and its land. The response from the public has been enormously encouraging, and another twenty-two acres of land have just been purchased. One old lady sent £10,000 when she heard what we were doing. Gradually, small sections of prairified landscape are being replanted with hedges, which will eventually, we hope, be as luxuriant as the one in the detail shown opposite, and broad headlands are being created at the edges of fields and sown with mixtures of wild-flower seed. The assumption is that there is no point in simply shouting at farmers to go organic. They will just ignore you. What you can do is to show that they can add to their farmed environment to make it more interesting, more varied, and to give a chance to the wildlife which can quite happily coexist with a farmer's business without doing any damage — easing the farming community into a more enlightened attitude. Birds Farm lies, like an oasis in a desert, in a part of the country that has been largely wrecked by arable farming. The hayfield that Robin and I opened a few years back was already ablaze with flowers last year — a delight to anyone who happened by.

Many, many people in Britain care deeply about their countryside. The trouble is, in my experience, that most don't get around to making a fuss about the activities and schemes that threaten it until the damage has been done. I am delighted that near where I live, for instance, big holes that were burnt out of the hedgerows are being replanted with hawthorn, but this should not have been necessary in the first place.

A host of English artists owe their inspiration to this country's landscape. The least we can do is to make every possible effort to protect it from the abuses it suffers and to shout from the rooftops when we see things going wrong. Not the least of the problems is sheer ignorance. Many local authorities, which have such a say in what happens to our surroundings, are woefully ill-informed about environmental matters. Artists are trained to be observant. Maybe that makes them well placed to blow the whistle.

Recently it has been brought home to me how very important the natural world is to all of us. Near where I live is a hospital where the imaginative attitude of the staff and people running it really touched me. For they have realised something that becomes extremely clear to anyone who has suffered serious illness and has to undergo long spells of treatment or convalesence: that when you are finding life really difficult, it is often nature that can calm and soothe most effectively. The wards are full of much-thumbed books about the countryside and about painters of the English landscape, indeed the wards are actually named after artists.

When I was asked to open a ward at Stoke Mandeville Hospital, I accepted the invitation with alacrity. The appreciation of art and nature here points up the fact that it is not just the people who are committed to the conservation of the countryside who discover that they care about it. Deep down, almost everyone has a need to know that they live in a world where the natural landscape and everything that belongs in it can flourish, where the seasons change and unfold in all the richness that has so excited artists over the centuries. If the countryside is harmed, it diminishes not just the natural world, but the quality of all our lives.

The landscape on the left is a Hertfordshire scene near Denham. The Norfolk vista below is one that caught my eye as I went to visit Oxburgh Hall – of which more later.

Right: the opening of the Beningfield Ward, with Sister Rickett, at Stoke Mandeville Hospital, 16th August 1993.

This painting came out of a commission from the Hertfordshire Society who wanted to present their patron, Her Majesty Queen Elizabeth The Queen Mother, with a gift on the occasion of their Golden Jubilee in 1986. The idea was to give her a painting of a view of the Hertfordshire estate where she was brought up. When I went to discuss the matter with one of her relatives who lives there, we decided to find a subject that would not have changed over the last ninety years, something that she would recognise. Then I saw the old oak tree on the lawn, which must have been there for hundreds of years. At the garden party that was held to mark the presentation, the Queen Mother leant towards me and asked what I had decided to paint. 'Well,' I replied, 'I fancied the old oak tree.' 'That's lovely', she said, 'because when I was a little girl I used to have a swing in that tree'.

I couldn't stop talking. The Queen Mother has that effect on you – so kind, so sunny-tempered, even though she has to grace many occasions of this kind. The next time I met her, when the butterfly reserve was opened near Tring, she was just as charming: the Queen Mother, the owners who had donated the land and I all sat at tables in a little woodland hollow and had tea provided by the Women's Institute.

Knowing of the Queen Mother's enjoyment of wild flowers, I painted a collection of plants that used to be so common that you would trip over them in the countryside: foxgloves, ox-eye daisies, hawksbeard, red campion, meadowsweet, a little bit of thistle, and, of course, bluebells. Nowadays, you can still find them, but much less frequently. Nature reserves are of course very important, but we have to take care of the land outside them too.

St Ives

Now I look back on it, I am amazed at my own cheek, but when I was a young man, it seemed obvious that if you were really fired up by someone's work, if your own feelings about art connected with what they were doing, you went and talked to them. Back in 1958, my wife Betty and I were on our honeymoon in St Ives. Discovering where Barbara Hepworth lived was not difficult, so one day we knocked on her door. 'Can I help you?' she said. 'Well, I've come to see you' I replied. 'In that case you'd better come in', she said. And we became instant friends. Much of my sketching and exploration of the Cornish landscape was done with an artist and great friend, Brian Fensome, with whom I spent many hilarious hours. The trip down to St Ives for my honeymoon was the longest journey I had ever made, and memories of the train ride along the Cornish Riviera remain among my fondest. I revisit the place whenever I can, and still enjoy the same, wonderful view of the bay from the train as it nears the town.

Butterflies and Stamps

The paintings on these four pages are of the chalkhill blue, red admiral, brimstone and orange-tip butterflies. My interest in butterflies dates from the early 'seventies, when I was researching paintings of birds and mammals. I realised that people were mainly not aware of the extent to which these extraordinarily decorative creatures are threatened through losing their habitats. And so it came about that my first book was on British butterflies. After *Beningfield's Butterflies* appeared in 1978, I was approached by the Post Office to do some designs for stamps featuring butterflies. I had long been concerned about the falling numbers of these delicate and beautiful creatures and was not alone in feeling that the case for their protection had been overlooked.

Peacock

Chequered Skipper

Small Tortoiseshell

Large Blue

Buff Tailed Bumble Bee

Emperor Dragonfly

Stag Beetle

Wart-Biter Bush-Cricket

Seven Spotted Ladybird

The chance to do the stamps suddenly became an opportunity to bring the idea of butterfly conservation to an enormous audience – they would get into every home in the land. Sometimes things just feel as if they are falling into place of their own accord, and Peter Crawford, who produced a BBC series I was working on, *In the Country*, suggested that we do a programme about designing the stamps – still more of a chance to draw people's attention to the problems faced by butterflies. The lengths we had to go to in preparing the designs just went to prove the point.

We decided that I would paint two relatively common species – a peacock and a small tortoiseshell – and two rare ones. In 1979, the large blue became extinct in Britain; this was my choice of an example of butterfly loss. Dr Jeremy Thomas, who was studying the species, had a permit to bring back live specimens from the Continent for his research, and he kindly allowed me to spend some time with one of his finds. Happily, since this gloomy moment, the large blue has been reintroduced into this country, and seems to be gaining a toehold again. The chequered skipper had also disappeared in England, but a small number still survived in Scotland. So we flew up to a location just outside Fort William where I was able to look at living examples of a butterfly I hadn't seen in England since I was a boy.

The organisation which has done most to champion the cause of butterflies is, of course, Butterfly Conservation. Now the most influential wildlife protection group for insects in the world, it was for many years guided by Sir Peter Scott, as its President; I am very honoured now to be following him in this role.

In 1985, the Post Office commissioned a second suite of stamps, this time a variety of insects: the wartbiter cricket, the bufftail bumblebee, the emperor dragonfly, the stag beetle and the ladybird. The wartbiter cricket is extremely rare, and the stag beetle, which would once have been thought very common, is not in a happy position either. Its normal habitat is oak woodland, in particular, rotting timber, of which there is much less than there used to be. The dragonfly is an example of an insect we need to look after, even though it still exists in some numbers.

BUTTERFLIES OF MICRONESIA
OFFICIAL FIRST DAY COVER

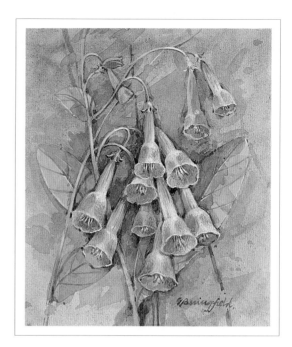

One of its main habitats is ponds, and over recent years thousands of these have been either totally filled in or polluted. I love to watch the dragonflies that flit up and down the riverbank near my home, which is fortunately the kind of place that allows them to thrive.

Back in the early 1980s, I was approached by Unicover, an American organisation in Cheyenne, Wyoming, to design a set of first-day covers showing butterflies. This was the first of many I have since done, including a series of endangered European butterflies. The pictures opposite were painted for first-day covers to accompany stamps depicting American orchids; they show the white fringed orchid and the lady's slipper orchid (top) and the spreading pogonia orchid and Pacific calypso orchid (bottom). The watercolours on this page are part of a series of fifty depicting the flowers of the American States. The top row are the meadow beauty (New Jersey), claret cup cactus (New Mexico) and Virginia bluebells (Virginia). Below are the shooting star (Illinois), rosebud orchid (Georgia) and jack-in-the-pulpit (North Carolina). Recently, I have even produced a set of four stamps, shown on the previous spread, of subjects for Micronesia. So stamp designing has become a fairly important occasional activity, though always concentrating on a natural history theme.

My first involvement with television was in the early 'seventies when it was suggested that I contribute to the BBC's *Look Stranger* series, describing what had led me from ecclesiastical art to painting the English landscape. Eric Morecambe, already a good friend and one of the kindest and funniest men I have ever met, provided the commentary to the programme, bringing to it his own deep love of the countryside.

Some years later the opportunity arose to take part in a number of editions of the BBC Natural History Unit's production, *In the Country*, and it was in the course of this that I met Phil Drabble. Working with Phil is always most enjoyable, and, because of my interest in sheep and shepherding, he later asked me to contribute to the long-running *One Man And His Dog* series.

The painting above was commissioned as a *Radio Times* cover to mark the twenty-fifth anniversary of the Natural History Unit. A montage of images seemed a good way of reflecting the sheer variety and richness of their output over the years.

Imax is a large-screen projection system, which has been introduced to special cinemas in North America and elsewhere, and, so far, to just one in Britain. Chris Parsons, whom I knew from the BBC Natural History Unit, made a film for Imax called *The Secret of Life on Earth*, about the origins of our planet and the chances for its continuing survival. To commemorate the film's world premiere in Toronto, I was asked to paint the picture opposite, which was then sold in aid of the World Wide Fund for Nature.

Thomas Hardy

Although my favourite novel by Thomas Hardy is *Far from the Madding Crowd*, *Tess of the d'Urbervilles* comes a close second. In the early 1980s, when I was preparing for my second major book, many hours were spent exploring Wessex. This part of the country was already pretty familiar to me – Dorset is certainly the part of England I enjoy most of all. One day, as I wandering around the countryside enjoying the sunken lanes and combes and high hedgerows, I came upon a gipsy family, with five attractive, dark-haired daughters, near their horsedrawn caravan travelling cross-country along what they called 'green lanes', well off the main roads. They could have stepped out of the last century, and I was mesmerised – reminded instantly of Tess. Several years later, I was lucky enough to meet Gertrude Bugler, the actress whom Hardy believed gave the best portrayal of his tragic heroine. Mrs Bugler was one of the most charming people I have ever had the privilege to meet, and we became firm friends. Over the years, we had long, fascinating conversations about her memories of Thomas Hardy. Yes, she confirmed, it probably had been the sight of her mother working as a dairy-maid in the watermeadows at Lower Bockhampton that Hardy had been thinking of when he created Tess. Her mother had long, luxuriant dark hair and was beautiful, just as her daughter was to be. Even as an elderly lady, Mrs Bugler had an entrancing face, and by the time I met her, although her black hair was by now pure white, it was still thick and elegantly arranged. Small wonder that the great writer held her in such regard. When my second book connected with Hardy, *Hardy Landscapes*, came out on the 150th anniversary of his birth, Mrs Bugler kindly inscribed my copy with the following words: 'If anyone asks you whether you knew Thomas Hardy, say, Yes, he was my friend,' she quoted him as saying, and continued,

'Through him came many friends. I am very proud to say Gordon Beningfield is my friend.' Since her death in 1993, I have missed Mrs Bugler greatly.

The painting above depicts the area around Tincleton, the Valley of the Great Dairies, where Tess spent the happiest days of her life being courted by Angel Clare, and the sheep opposite are grazing in the churchyard of Stoke Abbott, a village in the Marshwood Vale – another scene that seemed imbued with the spirit of Hardy.

As the years have gone by, I have grown to love the work of many artists, especially the Victorian watercolour painters who tended towards natural history subjects. Archibald Thorburn was and is a great favourite. But the painter who remains my greatest source of inspiration is Turner. It was when I was twelve that my headmaster suggested I look at Turner's work in the Tate Gallery. I was spellbound. Here was a painter whose work was far from literal but whose

imagination spoke straight to me. I knew what he meant; I could see what he was saying. Whenever I have a moment to spare in London, I spend an hour or so in the National Gallery, or the Tate, renewing my acquaintance with some of his pictures.

The way I paint in watercolour developed from the work I did in oil paint during my time at Faithcraft, when I used to prepare surfaces with a pure white oil colour, then glaze it with oils to achieve an effect of transparent brilliance. Some of the Victorians used body colour under watercolour for this very reason, to create a sort of luminosity, and this was the path I followed. Not a fashionable one, it has to be said, and my lectures have often been interrupted by people taken aback at the mixing of media. This is something they have been told never to do by their art teachers, but you must find the way of working that suits you. Whoever produced good work by just sticking to the rules?

I start off with a cream paper – one that was found when I was beginning to put together my first large-scale book, *Beningfield's Countryside*. First, I apply watercolour washes, very wet, very free, very loose, to begin to hint at the illusion I'm after. It's a nerve-racking process, because watercolours are tricky to manipulate in this way, but you have to work broadly and confidently to get as fresh and direct a result as possible. This is the moment for vigorous expression so that you have something live to build on. It is this stage which will decide whether the painting later comes alive, or looks stunted and laboured. Gradually the images, the shapes in the painting are worked up, wash by wash. As one dries, more watercolour tone is applied over the top of it. Sometimes the sable brush is wrecked by all the scrubbing and pounding that is done to work the colour in. Then is the moment for the application of gouache in the areas that need emphasis. To take an example, in the lambing yard painting on the next page, there is body colour under the sun, the sheep, and at the open door of the shepherd's hut. When I was applying

the yellows and oranges and greys in washes for the sky and background, the colours were moving all over the place and I dropped a chunk of body colour in for the sun, mixing it with the watercolour. This is what alarms people – 'It'll move!' they say. True. Either you catch it before it moves, or you move with it. The wetness is useful to me because I don't want hard edges. It allowed me, for instance, to take a brush and just drag it through the sun to get the thin, wispy atmosphere around it. The middle ground is the next area to concentrate on, but all the time I am working over the whole picture. Some artists work from, say, the bottom left corner of a canvas, completing every detail before they move on to the next section. I don't know how they do it. For me, the view of the whole painting coming gradually into focus is essential. Soon, some of the less pronounced parts of the picture can be left, and some will need a bit more working up. Finally, I might flick in the odd highlight here and there.

Sheep and Shepherds

Horn lanterns were used by many country people, but especially shepherds. The translucent parts were made of horn, rather than glass, making them much more durable and liable to survive being knocked over.

The picture on the left always reminds me of Gabriel Oak and *Far from the Madding Crowd*, even though the reference material for it came from Hertfordshire. This is a lambing fold built by a local shepherd called Alan Lungley, whom I have known for many years. For six weeks or more every year, he lived in his shepherd's hut tending the ewes and looking after the lambs. The actual enclosure is made of everyday rustic timber, then faced with hurdles and finally thatched with straw. Whichever direction the prevailing wind was coming from, the sheep could tuck themselves under the eaves for protection. Inside the shepherd's hut, Alan would care for

any lambs that needed extra attention. He used to tell me that the minute he tried to snatch a bit of sleep, they'd start galloping up and down the hut and nudging his arm for the milk that was kept warm on the stove night and day.

The sheep shown above have escaped into a bluebell wood and were on a farm very close to my home. The owner of the land and his family wanted to commission a painting of a scene they knew, and this one seemed to me so quintessentially English that I chose it straight away.

It was many years ago that I first became interested in the work and lives of shepherds before the Second World War. Inevitably, this focused on the South Downs, where sheep farming was for so long of enormous importance. A friend of mine, knowing that anything to do with shepherding fascinated me, handed me a little book called *Bypaths in Downland* by Barclay Wills. Never having heard of him, I glanced through the pictures of sheep bells, shepherd's crooks and so on, and then idly began to read. I was hooked. The descriptions of the life of downland and the shepherds who depended on it were so fresh, so evocative, that they made me want to rush down there and then and try to find some of the things Barclay Wills was talking about.

Here is a group of Southdowns that would have been an extremely familiar sight to Barclay Wills on his walks through the Sussex countryside. They were the predominant breed in this part of England in the early part of this century, and were famed for the quality of the lamb they produced. Their shape and the appearance of their faces are highly characteristic – short and broad, with small, rounded ears, and they are descended from the long-legged, grey-faced sheep that had lived on the downs for centuries before the breed was developed some two hundred years ago.

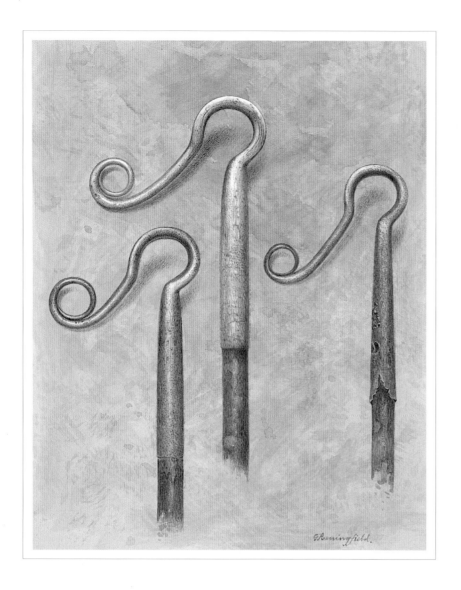

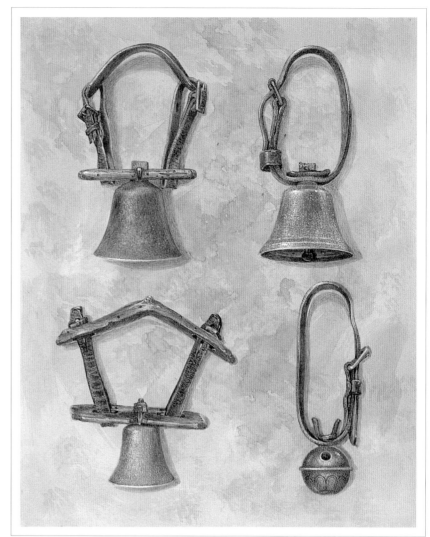

Over the years, Barclay Wills put together a considerable collection of shepherding paraphernalia – much of which was described in his books. I wondered where this was, and made various inquiries, but could find no trace of it. Then, after seventeen years, I discovered that the whole collection was in private hands in Kent. The family kindly allowed me to examine these wonderful objects and to make these detailed studies – it seemed to me important to document them very exactly, and catch the smell of them in a way you can't in a photograph.

The three iron crooks are all from Sussex. The middle one was owned by Barclay Wills's favourite shepherd and personal friend, Nelson Coppard, who later presented it to Wills. It was made in 1903 at a small downland forge in Kingston-by-Lewes. In a nice variation on the idea of turning swords into ploughshares, this crook was fashioned from an old gun barrel. The example on the right of the picture, a Pycombe hook, was made at Pycombe forge near Brighton; that on the left was forged by Mr Green, the blacksmith at the village of Falmer.

The four bells on this page were originally part of Barclay Wills's collection, and now I am lucky enough to own them. These all started as horsebells; they would have been part of a frame that stood off the collar of a heavy horse and were later converted to be sheep bells. The two on the left have chinboards made of oak, and a yoke. Top right is a white latten bell, which still carries Wills's handwritten label that reads 'formerly in hoods (sets) used on horses on timber waggons.' The round bell is a small crotal or 'rumbler' that came from Falmer and was made by Robert Wells, a bell founder.

On this page is the cream of Barclay Wills's collection. All except the bottom left bell (which is a clucket) are canister bells. The wooden yokes were carved by shepherds from odd bits of timber they picked up in the countryside, and the straps were recycled from old harness, probably cadged off ploughmen; you can still see the odd trace of colour on the yokes. These examples probably date from the eighteenth and nineteenth centuries. Shepherds were proud of their 'ring of bells', and sometimes a skin of brass was applied to add tone to the sound. But the bells also had an important practical function. On foggy days, which are not uncommon on the downs, if a good proportion of a flock was wearing bells, the shepherd would be able to rest assured that they were all safe by the sound they made. If they were disturbed for any reason, he would immediately know about it.

Oxburgh Hall

I well remember how my father used occasionally to talk about his 'ancient family'. How I wish now that I had listened more closely and could ask him about it. Shortly after *Hardy Country* was published, I received a letter from the College of Arms; it was from Henry Bedingfeld, York Herald, saying that he thought there might well be a connection between our respective families. Fascinated, I travelled up to the College, which I already knew well from heraldic research carried out for my work with stained glass. Henry and I got on well. He felt sure that if I could find the time to investigate my family history, we might discover that we were related. The idea was intriguing, but the thought of all the research that would be needed was daunting. Within weeks, and quite coincidentally, I discovered that a cousin of my father, Edward Beningfield, had been working away at the family history and was corresponding with a distant relative, Ron Hickman (the inventor of the famous fold-up Workmate workbench). He too had been tracing his way back through the generations, and had produced, in fine detail, a line that stretched back to 1066. Discovering that I was part of the old Bedingfeld family when I have always felt so drawn to England and its historical past was a great thrill.

The Hall dates from 1482, when Edward IV granted Edmund Bedingfeld royal permission for the building with 'stone, lime and sand' and the fortifying with battlements of a manor house. The fortifications were all too necessary in those lawless times, just to protect the inhabitants and their possessions from bandits. Much of the original building remains, and it makes an imposing sight rising up from the flat Norfolk landscape.

Dogs and Horses

Ever since Betty and I married, we have had dogs around the house. I'd always known about the ancient breeds of dog in this country, and used to dream about one day having one, but had never seen one in the flesh. Then one day, at a game fair, I suddenly came face to face with a tall, grey, rough-coated dog. Straight away I knew that this dog, which I discovered to be a Scottish deerhound, was for me. I started inquiring about getting hold of one. Our first, Rory, came to us as a pup and grew into a spectacular specimen. He lived a life of ease and freedom in the countryside, and when we arrived at shows, rival exhibitors would say, 'Oh no, not you again, don't bring that dog in.' We won the Best of Breed at the Peterborough Three Counties and many other shows, but then didn't bother with any more – I knew he was a stunning dog. We didn't need to prove it to ourselves with prizes. His is the middle head in the picture. Our next deerhound was Bruce (at the top), again a quite individual personality, this time a big gentle clown. Robbie, who we have now, is again a dog with a sense of humour. Despite his nine years, he still leaps all over the place, does somersaults and heads a plastic ball round the garden. But you don't take liberties with him any more than you would have done with Rory, particularly if he doesn't know you. His head seems to me to be the most beautiful of the three. Deerhounds are enormous dogs, but they're careful. They don't damage the house. They've a long history of living indoors; they're not kennel dogs. If we had a lot of land, I would have many dogs living with us, but if I have only one, it has to be a deerhound.

The two horses are probably 25 or 26 years old, and we've had them for over twenty years. The Grey, called Rummy, is owned by our elder daughter, Sally, and Worthington is Sarah's pony. Both my children learnt to ride on these ponies, and dote on them.

I was commissioned to paint this garden by a famous writer who lives in Sussex and values his privacy. It is the first time I have tackled this kind of subject, so it was an interesting challenge. What I try to do when someone wants a very personal painting of this sort is to try to work out, to sense what it is that they want out of it. In this case, the painting needed to sum up the spirit of the garden as it has been created, so that the owner can pass this memory on through his family. I hope the picture has achieved this for him.